Lime Academy Parnwell
Putting Children First
Saltersgate, Parnwell, Peterborough PE1 4YH
01733 9

The Boy Who Cried BOY

The Wolf Who Cried Boy

Bali Rai

Illustrated by
Komal Pahwa

Collins

Contents

The village 2

The humans 4

The wolves 5

Chapter 1 7

The animals of the forest 16

Chapter 2 19

Meet a real Indian wolf! 30

Chapter 3 32

Chapter 4 44

The Boy Who Cried Wolf 54

Chapter 5 57

Meet a real Bengal tiger! 68

Chapter 6 70

Habitat loss 82

Endangered animals 84

About the author 86

About the illustrator 88

Book chat 90

The humans

Mani

Jeeva

The wolves

Minstrel

Noor

Chapter 1

Minstrel loved exploring the forest. He loved to run far and wide. He even ventured out of range, despite his mother's warnings.

"But I meet dragons and princesses," Minstrel often replied. "Witches and wizards!"

"Yes, of course you do," his mother would say.

Minstrel's imagination had no limits. He saw things other wolves did not see. Giant trolls disguised as trees. Elephants hiding in the tall grass. Mermaids instead of silvery fish. Minstrel was a storyteller. He liked to make things up. The elder wolves had another name for Minstrel. They called him Liar.

Often Minstrel would rush back to his pack, crying "danger, danger!". He would say that dragons were chasing him. Or an ogre with a giant boulder. It was never true.

"Some day you'll face real danger," his father once said. "But no one will believe you. And that will be the end of you."

"I'm only having fun," Minstrel replied.

"Fun is a great thing," said his father. "But you have to stop making things up."

Minstrel didn't listen.

Minstrel's pack lived deep in the forest, far away from humans and their villages and towns and cities. On one side, their territory was bordered by a river. On the other side, giant grey hills rose high into the white clouds. They lived together with two other packs, happily sharing the forest.

When Minstrel was just a pup, his grandmother had warned him about venturing too far from his family. "We never go to the riverbank," she once said.

"Why?" asked Minstrel.

"Because we cannot trust humans," she replied.

Minstrel had never seen humans. He had only heard stories about them. In his mind, they were monsters.

"We used to live beyond the river," his grandmother told him. "Then, one day, humans came. We had to run away."

"How did you get across the river?" asked Minstrel.

"We were lucky," said his grandmother. "It was a hot summer and there was a drought. The river level fell. We waded across the shallows and into the forest."

"Did the humans chase you?"

"No," said his grandmother. "They only cared about building a new village. But we lost our old home. Thankfully, the other wolf packs accepted us here."

Minstrel had always wondered what lay across the river. And, when he grew a little older, he forgot his grandmother's warning. Secretly, he would walk to the edge of the forest. There, he would hide amongst the trees and watch the river. He never saw humans. Just birds and crocodiles and deer. And once, a majestic old tiger, lying amongst tall grasses, and basking in the sunshine.

Now, Minstrel sat watching the river again. But something felt wrong. On a hot, sunny day like this, usually the other animals would lie on the bank, or dip in and out of the river. But there were no animals on the bank. And, in the river, the crocodiles floated, their eyes just above the water, scanning the riverbank, keeping very alert.

Minstrel crept closer to the forest's edge. A startled mouse squealed and scurried away.

Suddenly, there was a commotion across the water. A flock of swifts rose high into the blue sky, squawking. Monkeys shrieked warnings, and several deer scampered onto the bank and then darted away again.

"What are they trying to get away from?" Minstrel wondered aloud.

An unexpected boom of thunder made Minstrel jump. He closed his eyes, shivering and whimpering with fright. He sat perfectly still for a few minutes, as the thunder continued to boom and roar. Only, as the sound went on, Minstrel realised it didn't sound like any thunder he had heard before. Slowly, he opened his eyes. It wasn't thunder at all. It was monsters. Big monsters that moved slowly and belched white smoke. Each monster had round feet that turned. And riding on them were strange animals that stood on two feet and ...

"Humans!" Minstrel whispered, remembering his grandmother's warning. "Humans and monsters!"

He turned and fled, his heart pounding. He ran as fast as he could. He had to warn the others. They were in big trouble. They had to get away!

He crashed through the undergrowth, scampering down well-worn tracks, warning the other animals. "Look out!"

When he finally reached his pack, he was almost breathless. "I saw humans!" he cried. "Humans riding monsters! They're coming for us!"

The animals of the forest

muntjac deer

Indian swiftlet

mugger crocodile

Indian wolf

Bengal tiger

Chapter 2

Just like Minstrel, Mani loved exploring. He loved to walk around his village and into the forest, and even further, until he reached the riverbank.

His mother often warned him not to. "The river is full of crocodiles," she'd warn.

"I'm not afraid of crocodiles," he'd reply. "They are my friends. We sit and drink tea together."

"Yes, of course you do," his mother would answer.

Mani was also a storyteller. His imagination never stopped working. He was always inventing characters and adventures and drama. Village life was hard work, and often very boring. Making things up helped Mani add excitement to his days.

The other villagers were used to Mani's tall tales. "Another amazing story?" they would ask him. "More lies to tell?"

Mani would smile and tell them of the golden elephant he'd seen. He'd recount his journey to the sacred Ganges River, on the back of a giant eagle. How he had rescued a beautiful princess from the clutches of an evil sorcerer. Many of the elders would laugh. "You are such a liar," they'd tell him.

"But you love my stories," he'd reply.

His mother would often scold him. "One day, you'll really get into trouble and no one will believe you."

Mani nodded, but he didn't agree. There was no danger, he was perfectly safe. In fact, nothing ever happened, that's why he made up stories!

Most of the villagers were farmers. They grew crops to feed their families. Whatever was left, they sold in the nearest town. However, the soil had grown weak. Their crops often failed. And each year the summer grew hotter. The droughts led to much hardship.

"We'll have to create more farmland," Mani's father had told him. "Otherwise, we'll go hungry."

"But where will we find more land?" asked Mani.

"Down by the river, and across the other side," his father had replied.

Mani thought of the riverbank and the forest. *How could they farm in a forest*, he wondered.

"We'll have to cut down the trees, to make room," his father continued. "And build a bridge across the river."

Mani was troubled by his father's words. He loved the forest and the river. Where would all the wildlife go? Who would replace the lost trees?

Mani sat by the river, feeling sad. The riverbank was his special place. It was where he invented his best stories. The forest behind him was like a green cloak. It allowed him to hide from everyone else. Now, the trees were being chopped down. Huge trucks were arriving with bridge parts. He could hear their engines roaring behind him.

In the river, he saw the crocodiles lurking just beneath the water. They were watching everything change. Mani wondered if they were sad too. On the bank, the usual gathering of animals had vanished. The deer and muntjacs had scampered away. The honey badgers and otters, the peafowl, swifts and mongooses had all vanished. And amongst the tree branches, the monkeys and macaques shrieked and then fell silent. Their beautiful home was being destroyed. *And all because of us*, thought Mani.

He got up and started trudging back to his village, glancing across the river. Suddenly, he saw something move in the trees on the opposite bank.

"What's that?" he wondered aloud.

It was difficult to know. Probably an otter or mongoose. It moved again. Mani realised it was bigger than he thought. He wondered if it might be a tiger! But he'd never seen a tiger around here. Besides, this animal was grey. It hid amongst the bushes, watching the river. Then it moved slightly.

"No!" said Mani. "It can't be!"

It was a young wolf. The first that Mani had ever seen. Wolves had roamed the forest freely, until the humans came. Then they had disappeared. No one had seen a wolf in years. Yet, there it was, staring across the river.

Suddenly, it turned and ran.

"WOLF!" cried Mani, turning towards the huge trucks.

As the drivers got out, Mani continued to shout. "WOLF!" he yelled. "There's a wolf across the river!"

The men laughed at him. "There are no wolves here," said one. "You are mistaken, boy."

Mani hurried home. It was some distance, and he arrived breathless. "Mother! Mother!" he shouted.

"Mani?" she replied. "What's the matter?"

"I saw a wolf!" he explained. "An actual wolf, across the river!"

"But there are no wolves here," she replied. "They left a long time ago."

"I'm not lying," said Mani. "I saw a wolf! It was grey and – "

"Mani – " she warned. "Stop making things up!"

Meet a real Indian wolf!

30

- Indian wolves live to be around 5-13 years old.

- They are social animals and live in small packs of up to 8 individuals.

- Indian wolves are territorial but do not howl like other grey wolves to advertise their ownership of a territory.

- They are nocturnal, being active between dusk and dawn.

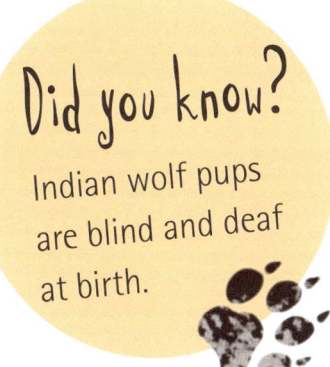

Did you know?
Indian wolf pups are blind and deaf at birth.

Chapter 3

One by one, Minstrel's pack began to laugh.

"I did see humans!" Minstrel insisted. "I did!"

The other packs joined in.

"You are such a liar!" said an elder wolf. "There are no humans here."

Minstrel looked at his mother. She shook her head in sorrow. "Oh, Minstrel," she said. "Why do you make up such stories?"

"But – "

"Enough!" growled Minstrel's father. "Go and sit, and think about your behaviour!"

Minstrel plodded away. The wolves' laughter echoed in his mind. He sat alone, away from the rest. With his head on his paws, he began to cry. "I did see humans," he whispered. "And they have monsters with them. Why won't you listen to me?"

A young female wolf padded over to Minstrel. It was Noor, his best friend. She had silvery fur with a black underbelly. She lay down beside him and nuzzled his head. "Please don't be sad," she told him.

"But they won't listen," sniffed Minstrel.

Noor sighed. "You're always making up stories," she said. "Why would they believe you?"

"Do you believe me?" asked Minstrel.

Noor looked away. "I don't know what to think," she said.

Her reply made Minstrel even more miserable.

Across the river, and through the forest, Mani was also glum. He sat under a mango tree, feeling sorry for himself. The other village children were playing all around him, but he didn't join in.

His best friend, Jeeva, sat down beside him. "Are you still upset?" she asked.

"Yes," he replied. "Why won't they believe me?"

Jeeva had long black hair and dark, shiny eyes. She put a hand on Mani's shoulder. "Because you always make up stories," she told him.
"Why should anyone believe you?"

"But I'm not lying this time," Mani insisted. "I'm not!"

"The wolves vanished years ago," said Jeeva. "Long before we were born. Why would they suddenly come back?"

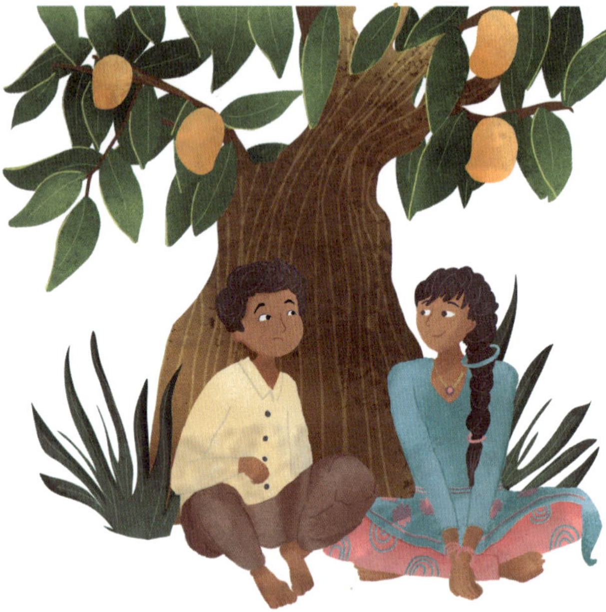

Jeeva's mother was not a farmer. Instead, she worked many miles away, in a big city. She was a scientist, and she worked to keep wild animals safe. So Jeeva knew all about wolves and tigers and other rare creatures.

"Perhaps they moved there when our village was built?" said Mani.

"But you always sit by the river," Jeeva replied. "You would have seen them before."

"Not if they were hiding," Mani pointed out.

Jeeva wondered if she was wrong. Was Mani actually telling the truth this time? Her mother was at home. She would be the best person to ask.

"Let's go and see my mother," she suggested.

"Why?" asked Mani. "So she can scold me too?"

"Because she knows about wolves," Jeeva replied. "Come on!"

Jeeva's mother was boiling milk when they arrived. Jeeva's family lived in a bungalow. It had a wide courtyard, with a low stone wall. The boiling pot sat on an open fire.

"I'm making tea," she told Jeeva and Mani. "Would you like some?"

They nodded and sat down. Jeeva's mother added tea and sugar to the milk. She also added spices – fennel seeds and cardamom pods.

"You seem sad, Mani," said Jeeva's mother. "What's the matter?"

"Haven't you heard?" he asked. "I've been accused of making up stories."

Jeeva's mother smiled. "But you always make up stories," she replied. "What's different this time?"

"Mani thinks he saw a wolf," Jeeva explained.

"A wolf?" Jeeva's mother repeated. "Here, in the village?"

Mani shook his head. "No," he said. "Across the river."

"That's very strange," Jeeva's mother replied. "Are you sure?"

"Yes," said Mani. "It was young and had grey fur."

"Young?" asked Jeeva's mother. "That means it belongs to a pack. That's very interesting."

"So, you believe me?" said Mani, feeling slightly better.

"I'm not sure," said Jeeva's mother. "You do make up some amazing tales, Mani."

Mani felt sad again.

"But there's nothing wrong with using your imagination," said Jeeva, hoping to make him feel better.

Her mother nodded. "All humans love a good story," she added. "Just make sure you let people know which are tales and what is real."

"I'm worried," Mani told her. "The forest is being cut down. The wolves will suffer."

"I know," said Jeeva's mother.

"Can we save them?" asked Mani.

Jeeva's mother shrugged. "I'm not sure," she replied. "Wolves aren't protected but we should try. Two or more tigers would be protected straightaway. It's the law."

"Really?" asked Mani.

"Yes," said Jeeva's mother. "But we'd need at least *two* tigers."

When the tea was ready, she poured three cups. The tea was hot and sweet, with a touch of spice. Soon, Mani felt much better.

Chapter 4

The next morning, Minstrel was determined to prove he wasn't lying – he really had seen humans! He crept away from his pack and set off for the river. He followed his usual tracks through the undergrowth, but it was slow going. The forest grew rapidly. Many of the trails he had created disappeared within days. Luckily, Minstrel was used to the forest. It was his domain. He used his scent, and the direction of light, to guide his journey.

Soon, he arrived at a clearing, where he stopped to rest for a moment. The river was not far now, but Minstrel still didn't have a plan. He wondered how he would prove that humans were at the river. Could he take something that belonged to them – something they wore or ate? Only, that would involve crossing the river. And Minstrel could not risk that. The humans might capture him. Or, he might get eaten by crocodiles, perhaps even drown.

He grew anxious and lay down. He had no idea how to prove his story. A cracking sound nearby made him sit up, his ears alert. His heart started beating faster. There was something out there. He took cover amongst some thick bushes and waited ...

Mani awoke before dawn and crept out of the village. He was determined to prove that he really had seen a wolf! He hadn't gone far, when he heard footsteps behind him. He turned to find Jeeva smiling at him.

"I knew you would return to the river," she told him. "I want to help."

"But, you don't believe me," said Mani.

"I didn't say that," Jeeva replied. "I just don't know what to think."

"Do you believe me now?" asked Mani.

"Let's find out," said Jeeva.

They walked for an hour, before they reached the riverbank. Dawn was breaking, and the bank was deserted.

"Look!" said Mani.

The builders had already begun to construct the bridge. Three metal supports rose out of the water.

"How can they build it so quickly?" asked Jeeva.

Mani had no idea. "I don't know," he said. "But I wish they would stop."

As the gloom of night lifted, Mani looked across the water. "We need to cross the river," he said.

"But how can we?" asked Jeeva. "It's dangerous!"

Mani had already spotted the answer. He pointed at a small rowing boat, tied to a wooden post. It belonged to the bridge builders. "There," he said. "We'll take that."

Jeeva followed Mani cautiously. "If the crocodiles eat me," she joked nervously, "I'll come back and haunt you as a ghost. I promise!"

Mani smiled. "We'll be fine!" he said. "Come on!"

The crossing was quick and easy. Jeeva kept her eyes closed, convinced that crocodiles would attack the boat.

"Don't worry", said Mani. "I've heard that crocodiles mainly hunt at night so they'll be asleep by now. Look, the sun is rising."

"But you saw them in daylight!" replied Jeeva.

"True ... well, even if the crocodiles are about, you probably won't taste very good," grinned Mani. "I'm sure they would just spit you out!"

Jeeva punched his arm in protest. Soon they were across the river and dragging the boat up the riverbank. Then, they set off into the forest.

When Minstrel saw his grandmother,
he gasped. "How can you be here?" he said.
"You passed away. I saw you!"

His grandmother approached and nuzzled
his neck. She was twice Minstrel's size, with
pure white fur and icy blue eyes. "Oh, Minstrel,"
she replied. "I am a spirit. I live in the other
realm now."

Minstrel had heard of the spirit world.
The place that all wolves went to, when they died.
But he had never believed the stories.

"But why are you here?" he asked.

"Because you are right," his
grandmother replied. "Humans are coming,
and the packs are in danger. I have returned to
help you."

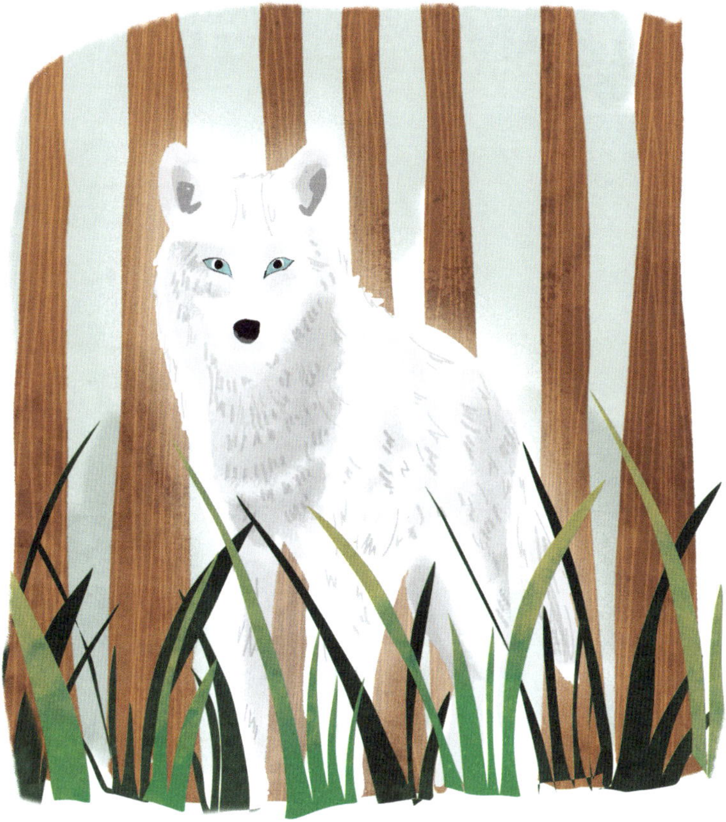

"Help us?"

"Yes," said his grandmother. "Two young humans are looking for you."

"To capture me?" asked Minstrel.

"No," she replied. "They are trying to help, too."

"I don't understand," Minstrel told her. "How can you know this? And why would humans help us? You taught me they were evil."

"Not all of them," said his grandmother. "Some of them are good. You must assist them, when they arrive."

"But how can I?" said Minstrel.

He was bewildered now. He was a wolf. They were humans. He couldn't communicate with them.

"You can," said his grandmother, reading his thoughts. She found a lilac flower amongst the bushes and brought it to him. "Eat this, Minstrel," she said. "Then you will understand them."

"But – "

His grandmother nuzzled him again. "Eat, Minstrel," she said. "You have a lot to learn – "

The Boy Who Cried Wolf

- The original story that this story is based on is called *The Boy Who Cried Wolf* and is over 2,500 years old! It comes from a collection of fables by Aesop.

- The original fable is about a shepherd boy who keeps tricking villagers into thinking that a wolf is attacking his sheep so they run to help. He tricks them so often that when a wolf really does attack his sheep they don't believe him.

The Boy Who Cried Wolf by Francis Barlow in 1687

- In some versions of the story the sheep all get eaten by the wolf.

- A fable is a story that teaches a lesson or a moral.

the front cover of an Aesops Fables book from 1672

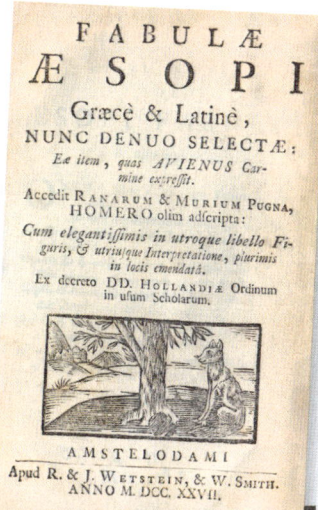

The Wolf and the Lamb by Jean-Baptiste Oudry in 1751

55

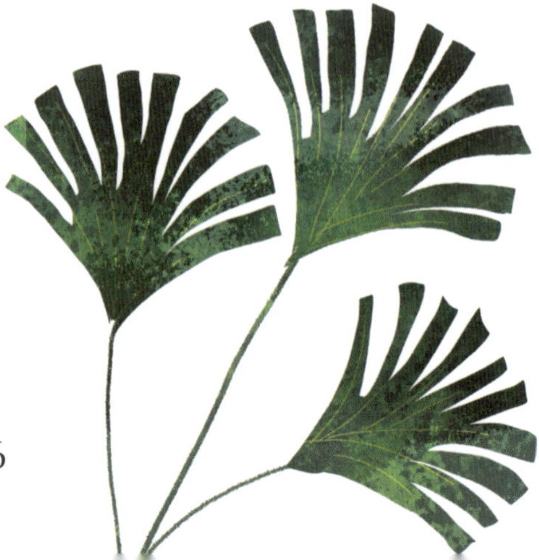

Chapter 5

Jeeva saw it first. A huge female wolf with pure white fur. Jeeva froze in fear.

Mani wasn't paying attention and bumped into her. "What are you doing?" he asked.

Jeeva pointed into the undergrowth. The forest was dense and dark, and it was hard to see. Yet, in the gloom, Mani saw the wolf too. She was magnificent.

"Don't move," Jeeva whispered.

"Should we just wait to be eaten?" replied Mani.

The wolf looked directly at them. Another wolf appeared behind her. This one was young, grey and male.

"They've seen us," said Jeeva. "What shall we do."

"Run?" Mani suggested.

"DO NOT RUN!"

Mani and Jeeva looked at each other. They had both heard the white wolf's voice, but neither could believe it. It was impossible.

"She spoke to us!" said Mani.

"Yes, she did," said the younger wolf. "I am Minstrel, and this is my grandmother, Taya."

"I'm Jeeva, and this is Mani."

Both wolves padded over and stood beside the humans. They did not snarl or bark. They did not attack.

"You are perfectly safe," said Taya. "We will not harm you."

Mani relaxed just a little.

Jeeva stood in shock, her mouth wide open. "How can you speak to us?" she eventually asked.

Taya nuzzled Jeeva's legs and Jeeva shrieked.

"We wolves have our own magic," Taya told Jeeva. "Just as humans have theirs."

"But magic isn't real," Jeeva replied.

"And yet, here you are," said Taya. "Speaking to a wolf spirit."

Taya asked them to sit, as she explained everything. How she had sensed danger and returned from the spirit realm. How she knew forest magic. "When your village was built, we had somewhere to go," she told them. "Our pack escaped across the river. This time, we have nowhere left to run. This time we must act."

"So, how do we save the forest?" asked Mani.

"That, I do not yet know," Taya replied.

"If only tigers lived here," said Jeeva.

Minstrel and Taya glanced at each other.

"Tigers?" asked Minstrel. "Why tigers?"

Jeeva told them what her mother had said. "Tigers are protected by law," Jeeva explained. "If they lived in this forest, it couldn't be destroyed."

Minstrel's eyes grew wide. "There *is* a tiger here," he told them. "An older male tiger. I saw him by the river, once."

"That can't be true," said Mani. "I sit across the river all the time. I've never seen a tiger."

Minstrel growled softly. "I'm not a liar!" he protested.

"Nor am I!" replied Mani.

Taya and Jeeva looked on in amusement, and both smiled.

"He was old," said Minstrel. "And he had a scar – "

"On his flank?" said Taya. "Long and thick, as though he'd been caught in a trap?"

"Yes," said Minstrel. "But how could you know that?"

Taya's blue eyes sparkled. "Because I knew him," she replied. "When I lived in this world. Is that old fool still alive? Wait here – "

Then, without another word, she left.

Taya soon returned with a tiger. A powerful beast. It was large, with a scar on his flank, massive feet and a gigantic head.

"Meet Arul," she said. "Arul, be nice."

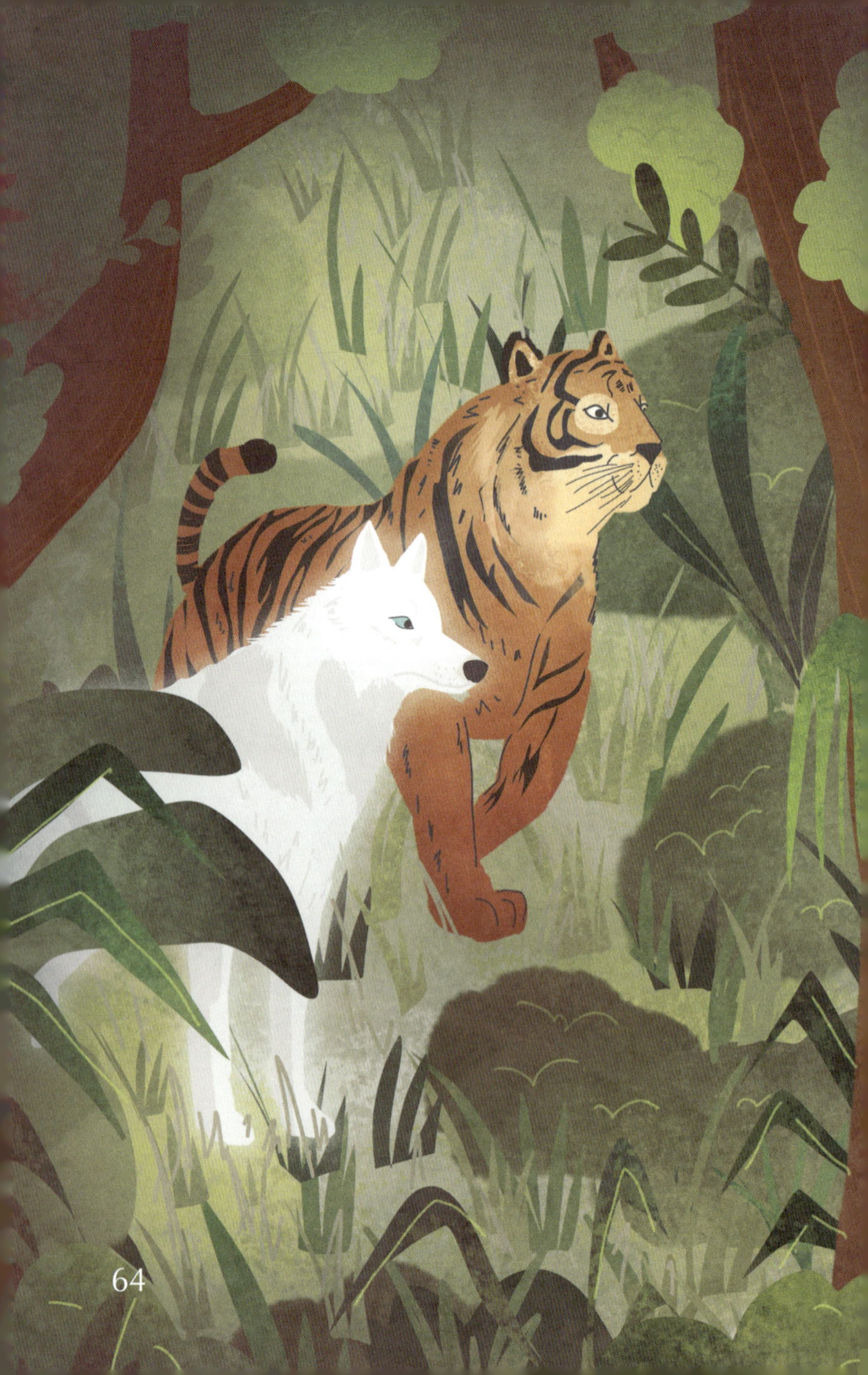

The tiger eyed Mani and Jeeva, then snarled.

Mani yelped. "It won't eat us, will it?" he asked.

"I would like to, human," Arul replied. "But Taya has made me promise not to."

The elder wolf and the tiger roared with laughter.

"This day is getting stranger by the minute," said Jeeva.

"Return to your village," Taya explained. "Tell your mother a tiger lives in the forest. Bring her back tomorrow morning. She will see for herself."

"She said two or more tigers," Jeeva explained. "The law doesn't work for a single tiger."

"Well, I'm the only tiger in this forest," said Arul.

"It seems we are stuck, then," Mani replied. "What shall we do?"

Minstrel considered things for a moment. Then he had a brilliant idea. "I have a plan!" he said. "We'll have lots of tigers come the morning."

"How?" Taya and Mani asked at the same time.

"Leave that to me," Minstrel replied. "Just bring Jeeva's mother to the riverbank by dawn."

Jeeva nodded, then she and Mani left.

"What's this great plan?" asked Taya.

Minstrel roared. It was a weak roar, but not bad.

"Can you do that?" he asked his grandmother.

"Yes, but – "

"Just trust me, please," said Minstrel. "But first we must return to the pack. I need you to speak to them."

Meet a real Bengal tiger!

- A male is called a tiger and a female is called a tigress.

- Bengal tigers can grow up to 9 feet long.

- They are very good at swimming.

- Bengal tigers tend to live alone or in small groups of 3-4 tigers.

- They make lots of different noises to communicate, they roar, grunt, growl, hiss, chuff and snarl.

Did you know?

Each tiger's stripes are unique – just like your fingerprints aren't the same as anyone else's!

Chapter 6

Mani and Jeeva reached the village and rushed to find Jeeva's mother. "We need your help!" they yelled together.

"Hold on," Jeeva's mother replied. "Where have you been?"

"We found the wolves," said Mani.

"They're real!" Jeeva added.

Mani was breathless. "And there's a t-tiger – " he panted.

"More than one!" said Jeeva, winking at him.

"Oh, yeah," he replied. "Loads of them – "

Jeeva's mother frowned. "Tigers?"

The children nodded.

"You have to come see them tomorrow," said Mani. "At dawn – "

"Right," said Jeeva's mother. "Calm down. Then tell me everything."

Minstrel's father nuzzled him. "I'm so sorry that we didn't believe you," he said.

"Don't worry," said Minstrel. "You do now."

Taya had explained everything. Now, as the wolves gathered, Minstrel outlined his plan. "You need to practise roaring," he told them all.

He showed them how. "Now your turn," he said.

One by one, the wolves tried to roar.

"No," said Minstrel. "Don't howl, roar!"

They tried again, and this time they were better.

"That's it!" said Minstrel.

Taya shook her head. "Now, that's a good way to use your imagination," she told Minstrel. "You clever pup!"

Minstrel grinned. Soon, he would go from liar to hero!

At dawn the following morning, Jeeva, her mother and Mani stood at the riverbank. Behind them, several village elders were also watching.

"There is nothing to see!" said one elder.

"Never mind this nonsense," said another. "We need to build the bridge and clear the forest. Stop wasting our time!"

Mani told them to wait. Then, as the sun began to rise, he spotted Arul across the river amongst the trees.

73

"There!" Mani shouted. "There he is!"

The elderly tiger stepped into view, and the human adults gasped. Arul stared towards Mani and Jeeva. Then he roared.

Suddenly, there was another roar, and then another, and then another.
Soon, the forest echoed with the sound.

"Amazing!" said Jeeva's mother. "Tigers!"

Minstrel and Taya stepped out of the shadows to join Arul.

"This is absolutely wonderful!" said Jeeva's mother. "They're standing together, to protect their home. Wow!"

Mani and Jeeva grinned at each other.

"This means nothing!" said an elder. "We must continue our work."

"You can't," Jeeva's mother replied. "The law is clear. Tigers are an endangered species. The forest beyond the river cannot be developed. Tomorrow, I'll register this land as protected. If you break the law, the penalties will be severe."

She turned to the children and smiled. "Well done!" she said. "You've saved a very important habitat."

"Thank you!" said Mani.

Minstrel was resting the next day, when the other wolves crowded round. He opened his eyes to see his parents. They seemed proud and happy, and he felt warm inside.

"We came to apologise," said his father. "We were wrong to dismiss your warnings."

"I deserved it," said Minstrel. "For making up so many stories."

"No," said his mother. "We were wrong for being so grumpy and serious."

"And look what happened," said another wolf. "You saved us, Minstrel. You saved the forest."

"What if they come back?" said Minstrel. "To look for tigers?"

Noor stepped away from the others. "They won't," she told him. "I went back to the river earlier. The monsters have gone. The humans, too. Except for your friends."

Minstrel wished Taya could have stayed.

"*That's not how the magic works*," he heard Taya whisper in his mind. "*But don't worry, Minstrel. I will watch over you, until you join me in the spirit realm.*"

Minstrel's best friend Noor nuzzled his neck. "Your friends *are* here though," she told him.

The wolves parted to create a path, and Mani and Jeeva stood smiling.

"Thank you for helping to save our forest," said Minstrel.

Mani crouched beside his friend. "I couldn't have done it without you," he replied. "I hope the forest is always safe. You shouldn't have to leave your home just because of humans."

Mani rubbed Minstrel's head and the wolf leant closer to him.

"He's just like a pet dog," said Jeeva. "Can we take him home? He's *soooo* cute!"

"No," said Mani. "He belongs here safe in the wild. They all do."

As Mani and Minstrel stood, the wolves began to howl in salute. Once they were liars. Now, they were heroes.

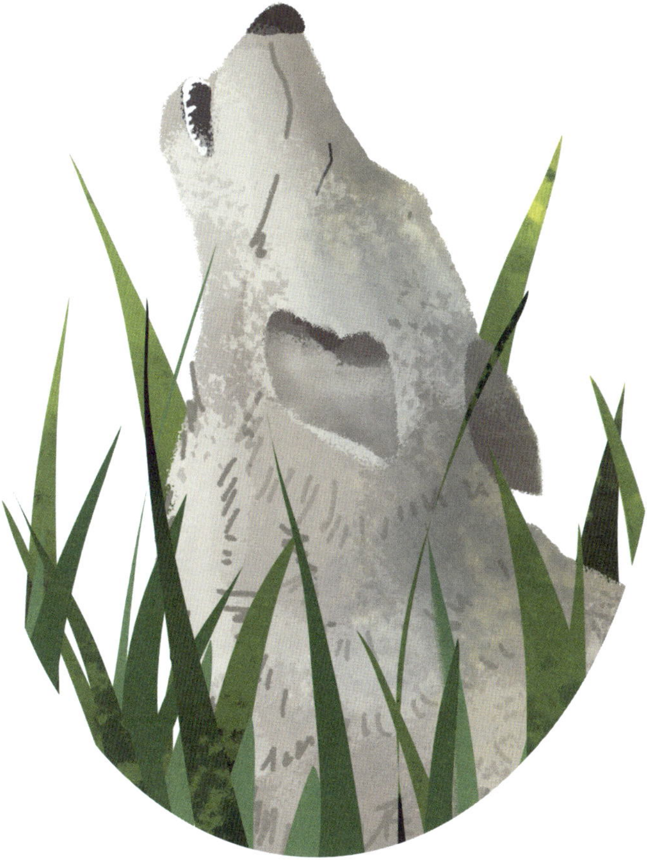

Habitat loss

In this book, Minstrel's forest is being affected by people cutting down the trees. This is known as habitat loss. Here are some more examples of habitat loss in the world, the reason why and the animals it affects.

Issue: Clearing land for planting
Habitat loss: Rainforests
Where: Borneo
Animals affected: Orangutans

Issue: Sea pollution and climate change
Habitat loss: Coral reefs
Where: Hawaii
Animals affected: Green turtles

Issue: Intensive farming
Habitat loss: Hedgerows
Where: UK
Animals affected: Hedgehogs

Endangered animals

Endangered means that a species of animal is at risk of dying out in the wild. Here are three categories for endangered species that experts use:

Critically endangered animals are at the most risk.

- Amur leopards – only 120 in the wild.

- Javan rhino – only 60 in the wild.

Endangered animals are becoming more at risk.

- Humphead wrasse
- Red pandas

Vulnerable animals could become more endangered if nothing is done to help them.

- Black spider monkeys
- Polar bears

About the author

Why did you want to be an author?

I was inspired by the books I read as a child – Roald Dahl, C S Lewis and others. Then, my hero, Sue Townsend, published *The Secret Diary of Adrian Mole*, and became my biggest role model. She was from Leicester, like me, so I wanted to follow in her footsteps.

Bali Rai

What is it like for you to write?

Writing is my passion. It allows me to get ideas and thoughts out of my head. It can be quite challenging, which I like, and sometimes even relaxing. It's part of my everyday life, and of me as a human being.

What book do you remember loving reading when you were young?

The first book I loved was *James and The Giant Peach*. I even wrote my own version of it, or tried to! I was a huge fan of the Narnia books too. Then it was Adrian Mole, which was set in my home city of Leicester. I loved that book, and still do.

Why this book?
The idea for this book came to me a long time ago. I always loved the Aesop fable on which this is based. One evening, I was watching a documentary on endangered species, which made me sad, and the idea developed from that emotion.

What do you hope readers will get out of the book?
I hope that readers will begin to ask questions about the effect humans have on wildlife and habitats. I also hope they will continue to imagine and make up stories!

What wild animal do you feel the most connected to?
It's very difficult to pick one, so I'll imagine that I'm seven years old again. Back then, my favourite animals were tigers – specifically Bengal Tigers, which once roamed across India. My family originate in the Punjab region of India, and told me many great stories about tigers and other animals.

Which wild place would you most like to visit?
Haha – that's too easy! I want to visit the Amazon. I have always wanted to go there. I've even been to Brazil for work, but still didn't get a chance to go. It's a place that excites my imagination, and I hope to visit one day soon.

About the illustrator

What made you want to be an illustrator?

Growing up I was always fascinated by Indian folktales and storytelling. I started drawing at a young age and entered art competitions. It became a way of expressing myself and connecting with people.

Komal Pahwa

What did you like best about illustrating this book?

I loved illustrating the characters specifically. This book felt very personal as if I was illustrating my cultural identity and roots. Villages in India are rich in cultural significance and history, and it felt like reminiscing about those beautiful vintage houses in the countryside while illustrating the scenes in the story. It felt very nostalgic illustrating a story from my country.

Is there anything in this book that relates to your own experiences?

The part where the mother makes tea in the backyard reminds me of a time we used to sit in houses like these and would just talk for hours and make up ghost stories to scare the other kids!

How do you bring a character to life?
I believe you have to become a part of the story. You must be able to think and feel what they would feel in different situations. Also, you have to understand the cultural significance and where they belong in order to communicate that.

Did you grow up in a city or a village like the children in the story?
I grew up in a city mainly, however, my grandmother and father used to visit their home village sometimes and I used to go with them. All that came back while illustrating this book and it felt very personal as well as emotional at the same time.

What did you find most fun to illustrate and why?
I loved illustrating the tiger to be specific, since I love them so much.

Which scene did you enjoy illustrating the most?
My favourite scene would be pages 34–35 where the characters are talking to each other in the back garden, I loved working on these pages. It felt like a scene from the past when I visited the countryside with my grandparents.

Book chat

Did you know the original fable this story is based on?

What do you think is the most important part of this story?

If you could change one thing about this book, what would it be?

What are the similarities between the wolf pack and the humans?

Which part of the book did you like best, and why?

What were the different moods and feelings you had when reading this book?

Which scene stands out most for you? Why?

Do you think Mani and Minstrel changed between the start and the end of the story? If so, how?

Book challenge:
Research an endangered animal and learn what you can about them.

Published by Collins
An imprint of HarperCollins*Publishers*

The News Building
1 London Bridge Street
London SE1 9GF
UK

Macken House
39/40 Mayor Street Upper
Dublin 1
D01 C9W8
Ireland

© HarperCollins*Publishers* Limited 2023

10 9 8 7 6 5 4 3 2

ISBN 978-0-00-862478-1

All rights reserved. No part of this publication may be reproduced, stored in a retrieval system, or transmitted in any form by any means, electronic, mechanical, photocopying, recording or otherwise, without the prior written permission of the Publisher or a licence permitting restricted copying in the United Kingdom issued by the Copyright Licensing Agency Ltd, 5th Floor, Shackleton House, 4 Battle Bridge Lane, London SE1 2HX.

British Library Cataloguing-in-Publication Data
A catalogue record for this publication is available from the British Library.

Download the teaching notes and word cards to accompany this book at:
http://littlewandle.org.uk/signupfluency/

Get the latest Collins Big Cat news at
collins.co.uk/collinsbigcat

Author: Bali Rai
Illustrator: Komal Pahwa (Astound Illustration Agency)
Publisher: Lizzie Catford
Product manager and
 commissioning editor: Caroline Green
Series editor: Charlotte Raby
Development editor: Catherine Baker
Project manager: Emily Hooton
Content editor: Daniela Mora Chavarría
Copyeditor: Sally Byford
Proofreader: Peter Baker
Cover designer: Sarah Finan
Typesetter: 2Hoots Publishing Services Ltd
Production controller: Katharine Willard

Collins would like to thank the teachers and children at the following schools who took part in the trialling of Big Cat for Little Wandle Fluency: Burley And Woodhead Church of England Primary School; Chesterton Primary School; Lady Margaret Primary School; Little Sutton Primary School; Parsloes Primary School.

Printed and bound in the UK by Page Bros Group Ltd

MIX
Paper | Supporting responsible forestry
FSC
www.fsc.org
FSC™ C007454

This book is produced from independently certified FSC™ paper to ensure responsible forest management.

For more information visit:
www.harpercollins.co.uk/green

Acknowledgements
The publishers gratefully acknowledge the permission granted to reproduce the copyright material in this book. Every effort has been made to trace copyright holders and to obtain their permission for the use of copyright material. The publishers will gladly receive any information enabling them to rectify any error or omission at the first opportunity.

p30 Danny Ye/Alamy, p54 The Picture Art Collection/Alamy, p55tr AF Fotografie/Alamy, p55bl Art Collection 3/Alamy, pp68–69 Puttachat Kumkrong/Shutterstock, p82tr Kjersti Joergensen/Alamy, p82bl RDW Aerial Imaging/Alamy, p83tl Shane Myers Photography/Shutterstock, p83tr Doug Perrine/Alamy, p83bl Juice Flair/Shutterstock, p83br Anne Coatesy/Shutterstock, p84tr tgladkova/Shutterstock, p84b InnovationWorld/Shutterstock, p85br Amazon-Images/Alamy, p85bl ILYA AKINSHIN/Shutterstock, p85cr Levent Konuk/Shutterstock, p85tl Tao Jiang/Shutterstock.